Searching for Sully's Enslaved

Beth Sansbury

Wolfe Hill Publishing
Great Falls, VA 22066
September 2022

ISBN 978-1-71661-878-9

Wolfe Hill Publishing
10850 Wolfe Hill Lane
Great Falls, VA 22066

Foreword

This is a tale of two stories in one book: the stories of the lives of those who were enslaved at Sully and the research paths that enabled me to discover what happened to them. The research story not only establishes the veracity of the facts presented but also lays out a path that might encourage readers to add content to these stories through their own research and family trees. I have also revealed my dead ends so that future researchers will know where to pick up the threads and push on to new discoveries.

The voluminous sources used in the book are not buried in footnotes but are presented as the story unfolds. Hopefully, I have given the readers enough information to check the sources for themselves if so desired. One type of source used throughout the section on the Richard Bland Lee family is a treasure trove of letters to and from the inhabitants of the house. They are available in the library at Sully. The originals are available in the Richard Bland Lee Collection, Library of Congress; Lee Family Papers, University of Virginia; Collins Family Papers, Library of Congress; and Parker Papers, Historical Society of Pennsylvania.

Two fellow docents helped me in this quest. Nanette Meo, through her experience with documenting her own family tree, was able to make important substantive contributions and was a good sounding board for ideas for future research. Bob Keegan, a lawyer in his former life, was able to interpret for me some of the more esoteric legalese of Richard Bland Lee's financial dealings and, through his volunteer work at other historic houses in the area, put me in touch with people who had relevant knowledge.

Beth Sansbury
Great Falls, Virginia

TABLE OF CONTENTS

Page

Introduction

In recent years much research has been dedicated to finding the descendants of the enslaved people who lived on the properties of historic houses in the American South. This book represents the first attempt to find descendants of those enslaved at the historic house called Sully in Fairfax County, Virginia.

The task was complicated by the tangled history of the house ownership. The man who had the house built, Richard Bland Lee, lived there from the 1790's to 1811. He was in financial difficulties for much of that time, which probably resulted in many of his transactions for the purchase or sale of enslaved to be hidden or unrecorded. A number of short-term or absentee owners lived at Sully after the Richard Bland Lee family. Very little was written about their enslaved people, but we know that various attempts were made to sell them in the deep South for work on sugar and cotton plantations where the use of enslaved labor was more profitable than for growing tobacco. It was not until 1842 that stability came to the farm again in the form of a Quaker family from Dutchess County, New York. Jacob and Amy Haight and their daughter and son-in-law, James and Maria Barlow, farmed Sully through the Civil War period. Despite Quakers' aversion to slavery, the families both rented and owned enslaved people at Sully. The Barlows—the elder Haights died before the war ended—sold Sully after the war and left for Kansas.

Because of the discontinuity of ownership at Sully, only a few of the lives of those enslaved can be traced to their freedom let alone to their present-day descendants. However, the stories of these lives shed light on the institution of slavery in Virginia and how other historical events impinged on this local history. They also fill in the lives of enslaved people who were often faceless and nameless. Hopefully, future research can expand their stories so that more of Sully's enslaved can be united with their descendants.

This book is a companion to "Sully Historic Site: The Story of the House and the People Who Called it Home." Both books can be found at Sully's Visitors Center and on Amazon.

Sully, as it probably appeared
when completed in 1795
Sketch by Mariano Eckert

Chapter 1: Enslaved People of Richard Bland Lee

This section attempts to provide a complete list of the enslaved people at Sully during the years that the Richard Bland Lee family lived there. This is the starting point for searching for their descendants. However, because these enslaved were property, this section is also the tale of the financial misfortunes of Richard Bland Lee and his futile attempts to get out of debt. He left a trail of financial subterfuge that affected his family most certainly but more poignantly uprooted the lives of the enslaved people in his keeping. For the latter, it was not only the economic uncertainty that accompanied being sold to new masters, but the emotional turmoil caused by family units possibly being torn apart.

Richard Bland Lee

A descendant of the famous Lee family of Virginia and Maryland, Richard Bland Lee was the brother of Maj. Gen. Henry (Light Horse Harry) Lee and uncle of Robert E. Lee. He came to his father's property, which later became his own, after leaving studies at William and Mary during the Revolutionary War. He first served in the Virginia House of Delegates from Loudoun County and then in Congress as Northern Virginia's first Congressman from 1793-95. Sully (the main house and some buildings) were built during the years he was in Congress, with his brother Theodorick acting as general manager. Moving to the District around 1815, Lee was appointed by his long-time friend James Madison to be one of the commissioners to superintend the reconstruction of Federal buildings damaged during the War of 1812 and after that, he was appointed a judge of the District's Orphans' Court.

Richard Bland Lee (1761-1827)
Virginia State Library, Richmond

His Enslaved People

The first enslaved people at Salisbury Plain, the property where Sully house would eventually stand, were placed there by its owners, Henry Lee I of Westmoreland County (1691-1747) and his son Henry Lee II of Leesylvania (1730-1787). The two Lees never lived at the property but owned and managed it; it was largely a tobacco plantation with overseers and enslaved. When Henry Lee II died in 1787, his estate deeded 3111acres jointly to sons Richard and Theodorick, each owning half, and Richard inherited 29 enslaved men, women and children.

Names and Monetary Value of the Enslaved Inherited by Richard Bland Lee
(According to the estate of Henry Lee II)

John of Henry	£80	Nancy of Prue	£20
Charles	£70	Henry of Prue	£15
Sam the Blacksmith	£80	Sally of Prue	£10
Pat	£60	Hannah of Lett	£10
Arthur	£50	Maskrell	£25
George of Nell	£50	Will of Franky	£25
Simon	£60	Old Eve	£ 5
Anthony	£50	Sam of Pat	£10
Tom Sorrel	£30	Nelly of Milly	£10
Lett	£40	Old Hannah	£ 5
Prue	£50	Cain	£ 5
Hannah of Hannah	£50	Old Dewey (of no value)	
Margery	£30	Anne of Lett	£15
James of Prue	£25	Tarpley	£25
Nancy of Franky	£30		

In 1792, after the death of Henry Lee's wife, Lucy Grymes Lee, the names of five more enslaved people and their values were added to the list owned by Richard Bland Lee:

Dick	£35
Winney	£30
Elliott	£10
Billy	£35
Betty	£30

Enslaved People Bought and Sold   □

In January 1809, about twenty years after receiving the enslaved people willed to him by his father, Richard Bland Lee had his lawyer draw up an indenture document, or deed (now in Historic Records Center, Fairfax County) that conveyed a list of his enslaved people to three associates to be held in trust "for the sole and separate use" of his wife, Elizabeth Collins Lee. These 29 enslaved people were probably those whom he considered the most critical to the running of his farm and household. They were:

John and his wife Alice and their children Patty, Betty, Henry, Charles, Johnny, Margaret, Milly and Frank

Ludwell and his wife Nancy and their children Caroline, Harriet, Frederick, Ludwell and Barbara

Henny and her child Eleanor

Rachel and her child Rachel

Two sisters Kitty and Letty and their brothers Alexander and Alfred

George (a blacksmith)

Thornton (a cook)

Samuel (a smith)

John (a ploughboy)

Two enslaved people, not in the above list but known because they were referred to in letters written to and from Sully, were Elliot (Patty's son) and Madam Juba. Elliot was mentioned in a letter written in 1802 by Elizabeth Collins Lee to her brother Zaccheus Collins in Philadelphia, and Madam Juba, a laundress, was mentioned in a 1797 letter from Thomas Shippen, a visitor at Sully.

Very few of the names in the 1809 indenture document above match the names of the 29 enslaved people that Richard Bland Lee originally inherited. Because twenty years had passed since the first list was drawn up, some of those enslaved inherited by Lee probably had died, but we do not know how many. No Sully records note the death of those enslaved, and no graveyards for the enslaved people have yet been discovered (see graphic and box below). Such a large turnover in the enslaved cohort suggests that Lee was continually engaged in buying and selling enslaved people. Some of these transactions were noted in court, tax, and land records but most were not. "Private sales" of those who were enslaved did not need to be recorded, a convenient way for slaveholders to avoid public disclosure. It was not until a "slave schedule" was mandated in the Federal Census of

1850 and of 1860 that the names of slave owners were included, but only the age and gender of those enslaved were recorded, not their names…and the Lees had left Sully by 1811.

Where did the Enslaved People Live?

The location of the cabins where Sully's enslaved lived was not known until extensive archaeological excavations were conducted beginning in the 1980s. The foundations of at least three dwellings within close proximity to each other were found along the newly discovered south road. Fairfax County Park Authority carpenters, with financial help from the Sully Foundation, built a structure on the middle foundation, which was completed in May 2000. It was built with period tools and techniques and measures 16' by 20', duplicating the archaeological footprint. It was built on stone piers, has oak log walls, a pine floor, a cedar roof, and a stone and brick chimney built from local field and sandstone from Cain's Branch, the stream that runs nearby through Sully property. An original large hearth stone can be seen at the front of the hearth. Probably not all of Sully's enslaved people were housed in these three structures. Some may have been housed in other outbuildings or in quarters out in the fields.

Although many archaeological discoveries were made during the excavations such as broken pottery and animal bones, which provided some evidence of day-to-day life, no evidence was found of enslaved burials. These possibly were further afield, perhaps on property now occupied by Dulles Airport.

To view a video of the reconstruction of their dwelling, see the Discovery Virginia website:
www.discoveryvirginia.org/islandora/object/islandora%3A11046

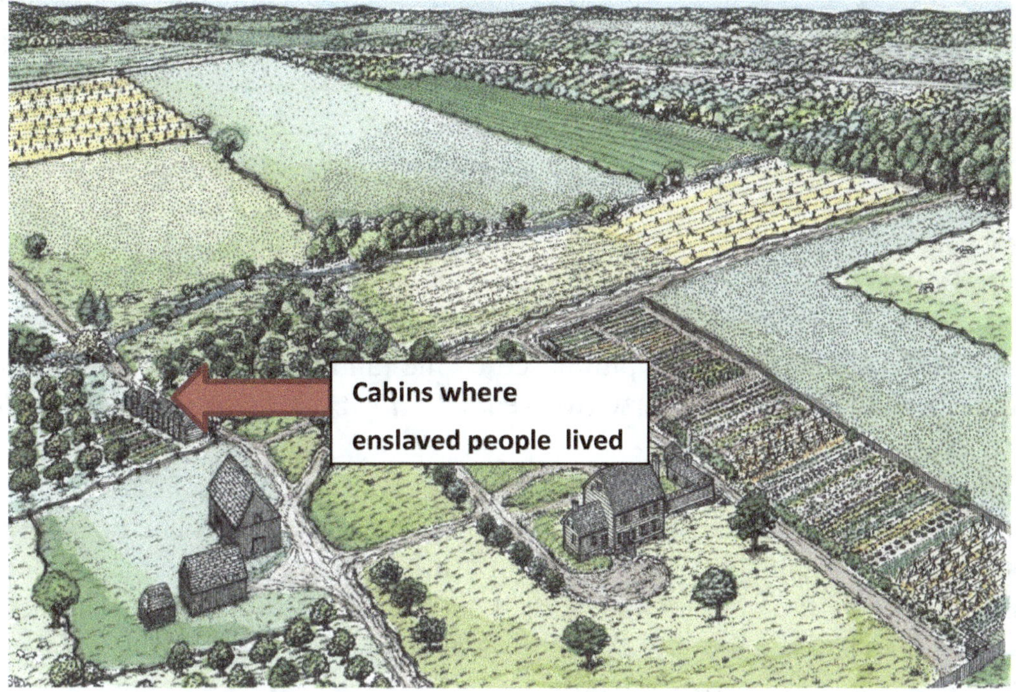

Fairfax County artist's depiction of Sully in the early 1800's
that hangs in Sully's Exhibit Room (tab added).

Tithables

During the years the Lees were at Sully, the Commonwealth of Virginia collected a head tax on "every free male person, above the age of twenty-one years…and also upon all slaves." These were called "tithables." Only numbers of enslaved people were given with no names attached. The following numbers were reported for Sully:

          1801 – 14 tithable "slaves"

          1806 – 14 tithable "slaves"

          1811 – 23 tithable "slaves"

The Federal Census of 1810 recorded "39 slaves" at Sully.

Listed below are the enslaved transactions of Richard Bland Lee that were officially recorded while he lived at Sully. This is probably not an exhaustive list.

- In October 1791 Richard Bland Lee "bargained and sold" to George Shiveley for one shilling "one negroe boy named Isaac aged about four years…" *At a court held for Loudoun County 10 February 1792*
- In February 1803 "at a court held for Fairfax County…Richard Bland Lee acknowledged this deed of manumission to Negro Henrietta to be his act and deed," having "served out the term stipulated at the time when purchased by me [and I] make free the said Mulatto woman slaved named Henrietta, aged forty two years." *Fairfax Deed at the Historic Record Center at the Fairfax Courthouse*
- In February 1803 "at a court held for Fairfax County…Richard Bland Lee acknowledged this deed of manumission to Negro Barbary to be his act and deed." The document further states that "a Mulatto woman slave named Barbara [different spelling than at the beginning of the document] aged eighteen years hath served out the term stipulated at the time when purchased by me [and I] make free the said Mulatto slave named Barbara." *Fairfax Deed at the Historic Record Center at the Fairfax Courthouse*
- On 22 April 1806 Richard Bland Lee and Nathaniel Pendleton of New York sold a negro man named Natt aged about nineteen years to Joseph Sewell for $349. *Historic Record Center at the Fairfax Courthouse*
- On 20 August 1806 Richard Bland Lee bought "a Negro woman named Rachel and her Child and their Increase" from Charles Little for $220. Rachel is probably the slave named in the 1809 document ("Rachel and her child Rachel"). *Historic Record Center at the Fairfax Courthouse*
- On 24 January 1807 Henry Lee of Westmoreland County sold to Richard Bland Lee for $2,000 the following slaves: Ozman, John, Reuben, Eric, Letty, Ester, and 1 male and 2 females, according to records in the *Sully Historic House library*.
- In March 1808 land and slaves of the late Thomas Lang of Botetourt County were conveyed to Richard Bland Lee to cover a debt owed him by Henry Lee. *Botetourt County Court Records: Deed Book 10, pp. 57-59.*
- A Virginia court document of January 1809 records that a slave named Milly "with her increase" was sold to John P. Van Ness of the District of Columbia. The phrase "with her increase" meant that any children that Milly had in the future would also belong to Van Ness.

- A Virginia court document of August 1811 records that Lee bought "a Negro man slave Peter" from Nicholas Peers of Leesburg.

Richard Bland Lee was a successful farmer, realizing that the days of monoculture were over and even trying experimental crop techniques, but he was a poor financial manager. For much of his life at Sully and afterwards, he was in deep financial trouble (see box below), confirmed both by him and his wife in impassioned letters to friends and family. Some of this problem was caused by his obligation to cover the debts of his brother, Light Horse Harry Lee, who went to debtor's prison, but much also was the fault of his own poor investments, such as in building the town of Matildaville with his brother on the ill-fated Patowmack Canal. Because he needed the money and his wife wanted to move closer to schools for the children, they moved from Sully in 1811 and settled finally in the District of Columbia by 1815. In the interim they lived in Alexandria and then moved to a country house called Strawberry Vale near present-day Tysons Corner.

Richard Bland Lee's Estate (death in 1827)

According to an inventory (in his own words) of Richard Bland Lee's estate given to the Sully Foundation by Eleanor Lee Templeman, the great-great granddaughter of Richard Bland Lee, the assets listed upon his death were largely aspirational rather than tangible and included no enslaved people.

- A house and lots in Washington valued at $8,000.
- A judgment against John Hopkins for $12,000 (Lee added the note "collectible?")
- Twenty-three shares of stock with an undecipherable name valued at $1150.
- Land on Bigbone Creek in Kentucky costing $5,000 but now worth $3,000.
- A life estate in the farm at Langley valued at nothing but perhaps someday accruing to $2,000.
- General Light Horse Harry's $40,000 bond and note possibly being worth $10,000. He added optimistically, "Should Genl. Lee's bond and note be rendered effective by a recognition of a claim held by his son for the benefit of his creditors on Florida lands, add $30,000."

Two Court Cases Against the Lees Involving Sully's Enslaved People

In January 1817 Richard Bland Lee took out a loan from the Bank of the United States for $6,000 ("renewable at the pleasure of the bank") and endorsed by Edmund J. Lee and Walter Jones. To further secure the repayment of money, a deed of trust was executed for eleven "slaves" and sundry household goods valued at $7,200 to Richard Smith, with power to the trustee to sell in default of payment after giving thirty days' notice.

The bank took a long time to realize—or act on the fact—that the loan had never been paid. In 1834 the bank filed a Supreme Court case (Bank of the United States v. Lee – 38 U.S.107) against Edmund J. Lee, Elizabeth Lee, and Richard Smith alleging that Richard Bland Lee died in 1827 intestate, that no one had administered his estate and that Elizabeth Lee had converted the "slaves" and household goods to her own use after the death of her husband. Elizabeth answered that the property pledged to pay the bank debt by her late husband had been conveyed by him in 1809 to Lee, Maffit and Coleman in trust for the sole and separate use of her (described above). The Bank claimed that it was unaware of the deed and, moreover, that Richard Bland Lee, at the date of the deed in 1809, was largely indebted and "incompetent in law" to make such deed for the benefit of his wife and family. The bank charged that the trustees had allowed Lee "to retain possession of the household goods" (that had been pledged with the "slaves" to secure the loan) "and to use, enjoy, and dispose of the same, and held himself out to the world as the true and absolute owner." Likewise, the suit accused the trustees of permitting the Lees "to bring the slaves and furniture from Virginia to the District of Columbia and county of Washington, about the year 1814, and there to continue his use and enjoyment of the same, as if he were the absolute, entire, and unqualified owner thereof."

Elizabeth Lee's lawyers asserted that Richard and Elizabeth had agreed that Richard should be authorized at any time during his life, to sell or otherwise dispose of any part of the "slaves" and furniture, with the consent of a majority of the trustees "provided the said Richard should convey to the said trustees…other property, real or personal, the full value of the said furniture or slaves, so sold or disposed of." Supreme Court documents show that trustee Edmond J. Lee sometimes prevented Richard Bland Lee from selling the enslaved, but at other times allowed such sales when other property of equal value was substituted. In one instance, "a new coachee horses and harness" were substituted. In another, a piano forte and a mantle clock were substituted for the sale of a "slave girl" named Milly. A document of 9 January 1809 noted that "Milly, a coloured slave girl, with her increase" were sold to John P. Van Ness, of the city of Washington and District…" At other times, it appears that Mrs. Lee's property was substituted when her husband sold the enslaved.

A complex deal involving a debt to George Washington's nephew Bushrod Washington, to be paid with the proceeds from the sale of some of Lee's land and secured by "eight slaves," was not completed, the court noting that the lands were not sold, yet "the eight slaves, who in such event were to be returned to her husband, had been disposed of by him." The named enslaved were Ludwell, Thornton, Henry, Butler, Tom, Samuel, Jack and Eleanor. Bushrod Washington was also on the Supreme Court that heard the Lees' case, although he was not on the decision. Another court document of August 1811 showed that Richard Bland Lee gave three hundred dollars "to be applied to carry into effect his contract with a certain Nicholas Peers of Leesburg, for the purchase of a negro man slave Peter…" and that Edmund J. Lee was holding the enslaved "as further security for a debt due to Mrs. Elizabeth Lee from Richard Bland Lee, her husband, amounting to ten thousand dollars."

Elizabeth Collins Lee (1768-1858)

Richard Bland Lee met Elizabeth Collins while he was serving in Congress when it was meeting in Philadelphia. Dolley Madison was a life-long friend of Elizabeth's, as they were both from wealthy Quaker families there. They were both expelled from the Society of Friends for "marrying out of the faith." Elizabeth exchanged life in the big city for life as a gentleman farmer's wife in rural Virginia. She admitted loneliness in letters but had her hands full, eventually with nine children (four lived to maturity), and a household to run. Despite her Quaker upbringing, she never openly questioned the institution of slavery. Apparently insensitive to the realities of life as an enslaved person, she wrote this to her brother after one of their enslaved escaped: "… true proof of the ingratitude of Slavery—too much indulged and his freedom promised in 6 years."

Although continually worried by her husband's indebtedness (he often sought loans from her brother), she probably was not privy to the subterfuges that resulted in the two court cases.

Elizabeth Collins Lee
Virginia State Library, Richmond

The Court ruled that because of a technicality, Elizabeth Lee was not guilty of fraud: "Mrs. Lee, with the ardour common to her sex, mistook her true interest in making the exchange of her land for the slaves and household goods; that she has been greatly the sufferer, is free from doubt. The Virginia estates have passed into other hands, to satisfy her husband's creditors: most of the slaves have been sold to supply his improvidence and necessities: and the little that is left of the property secured to Mrs. Lee (down to the humblest utensil) is now sought to be appropriated to the satisfaction of the judgment on which the bill is founded." The author concludes from this long complex legal tangle that most of the Lees' enslaved probably were sold before the Lees moved to the District of Columbia (see section on Ludwell for one possible exception). Most of them probably were sold to the next owner of Sully, Francis Lightfoot Lee, because the tithables list for Sully counted 23 slaves in 1817, the same number as in 1811. In 1820 Richard Bland Lee reported to the US Census taken in the District of Columbia that he owned only 4 "slaves"—1 male under 14, 1 female under 14, and 2 females 14-25.

The second court case involving Sully's enslaved (U.S. Supreme Court case Lee v. Lee, 33 U.S.8 Pet. 44 44) was filed against Elizabeth Lee in 1834. Samuel Lee and Barbara Lee, said to be formerly enslaved by Richard Bland Lee, filed for their freedom [enslaved with these first names were in the 1809 indenture document]. Their justification was that they had been born in the state of Virginia and enslaved by Richard B. Lee, "now deceased," who moved with his family into the County of Washington (District of Columbia) in about the year 1816, leaving the petitioners residing in Virginia as his enslaved, until the year 1820. Then Barbara was removed to the county of

Alexandria in the District of Columbia, where she was hired to a Mrs. Muir for a period of one year. The petitioner Sam was in like manner removed from Sully to the County of Alexandria and was hired by General Walter Jones for about five or six months. After the expiration of the said periods of hiring, the petitioners went to "the County of Washington" where they continued to reside as the enslaved of Richard B. Lee until his death, and since as the enslaved of his widow, Elizabeth Lee.

The petitioners claimed that they were taken to Alexandria with the intent to evade the law that prohibited the direct importation of enslaved people from Virginia to Washington D.C. but allowed them to be taken to Alexandria first and then to the other part of the capital, "the County of Washington." A Maryland law of 1796 made it unlawful to import or bring enslaved people into the state, and if it was done, the owner would lose all property rights and those enslaved would be free. An Act of Congress in 1812 seemed to reverse the Maryland law, making it permissible for enslaved owned in the Alexandria part of the District to be brought into Washington County without loss of ownership.

The court ruled for Mrs. Lee, deciding that there was no evidence of pre-intent to circumvent the law and therefore Barbara and Samuel were not free. We do not know what happened to Barbara and Samuel. The court case seems to be at odds with some facts as we know them. Richard Bland Lee sold Sully in 1811 to Francis Lightfoot Lee, and it seems likely given his indebtedness that he would have wanted to sell the enslaved as well. It seems unlikely, therefore, that two of his enslaved would have remained at Sully until 1820. James Sewall Morsell was a judge of the District Circuit Court at the time and before that, he was a lawyer who represented a number of African American families that petitioned for their freedom before the same Circuit Court. Of the three Circuit Court judges, Judge Morsell was the only dissenting vote in the decision for Mrs. Lee.

Enslaved People Sue Their Owners for Their Freedom

Freedom suits were filed in the Thirteen Colonies and the United States, a right descending from English common law. A web site called "O Say Can You See: Early Washington, D.C., Law & Family" (http://earlywashingtondc.org/) collects, digitizes and analyzes freedom suits filed between 1800 and 1862 in Washington D.C. The suit by Barbara and Samuel Lee against Elizabeth Collins Lee is included in this collection of nearly 500 petition cases. The reasons for filing were various, including wrongful enslavement after being held in a free state or after having served in the Revolutionary Army, being freeborn and illegally held in slavery, or a promised manumission that was not completed.

It is not clear who paid for this legal work. In Virginia, petitions for freedom were classified as "in forma Pauperis," meaning pleadings by persons without the means to otherwise bring a suit before the court. Some enslaved plaintiffs could have paid their legal fees, having earned wages from being hired out. Anecdotal evidence indicates that prominent lawyer Francis Scott Key did some pro bono freedom suits in Maryland. Maryland lawyers were paid a set fee by the court if the defendant slaveholder lost.   These men, who were often slaveholders themselves, may have been motivated by the desire to help codify the maze of laws that pertained to the enslaved in the various states and the District. Judge James Sewall Morsell, the one judge in the Lee case who voted in favor of the slaves' petition, owned 46 enslaved people in Calvert County, Maryland, according to the Federal 1850 Slave Schedule. When Judge Morsell was on the Circuit Court of Washington, his explanation for ruling for one of the enslaved plaintiffs was benevolent as well as racist. He wrote in Hillman vs. Moshier in 1850 that "negroes" could not be held to the same standard of legal vigilance as whites because "negroes [were] a class of people remarkable for being almost entirely ignorant of their rights."

Chapter 2: Descendants of the Enslaved People Owned by Richard Bland Lee

Most of the lives of the enslaved cannot be traced at all, but two (albeit one, Elenor Berry, probably never lived at Sully) can be traced to present-day descendants. Others can be traced to their next "masters" but the trail grows cold after that. The discovery of new sources of information in the future and/or family memories passed down to the present generation hopefully will expand the number found.

Elenor Berry

Elenor Berry, formerly enslaved by the Lees, wrote a letter to Elizabeth Collins Lee in 1827 from Chambersburg, Pennsylvania, mourning the death of Richard Bland Lee. In it, she thanked Elizabeth for "the way you brought me up for I am abbel to make my living" and drolly added, "I thought I was a slave when with you but I am a greater one now for I have twelve children and I have to work very hard to keep them."

The 1870 US Federal Census reported that Elenor Berry was born in 1784 in Virginia. According to a Chambersburg historian, she belonged to Henry Lee III (Light Horse Harry, Richard Bland Lee's brother) when his family lived at Stratford Hall, and she was a nursemaid to Henry Lee's son, Robert E. Lee, born in 1807. However, historians at Stratford Hall made a thorough search of the enslaved people there but could not find anyone named Elenor or a variation thereof when Light Horse Harry lived there. They said that it is possible that Harry and his wife Ann had an enslaved nurse that his family personally owned. No enslaved people belonging to Lighthorse Harry appear in the records at Fairfax County's Record Center. When Richard Bland Lee signed a long indenture document in 1809 that would convey his enslaved to Elizabeth Collins Lee if he died, 32 enslaved people were named, but Elenor was not one of them. A child "Elinor" was listed, but Elenor Berry would have been 25 years old by that time. None of the voluminous letters of Richard Bland Lee or Elizabeth Collins Lee mentions Elenor. The only information that ties Elenor as belonging to the Richard Bland Lees is her 1827 letter.

Research into the lives of Richard Bland Lee and his brother Light Horse Harry when both families lived in Alexandria produces a plausible story. Light Horse Harry was in continual debt to his brother. He moved to Alexandria after leaving Stratford Hall and might have sold/given Elenor to the Richard Bland Lee family when they all lived in Alexandria. Light Horse Harry's family moved to Alexandria in 1810 and Richard Bland Lee's family moved there in 1811. Triangulating further on this spot, Ferdinando Fairfax, the man who freed Dennis Berry, Elenor's future husband, also lived in Alexandria at the same time. Dennis was Ferdinando's postilion—a man who rides on the left front horse in a team of horses pulling a carriage. Driving Ferdinando around town would have provided Dennis with a good opportunity to meet other enslaved people. Ferdinando traveled in the same circles as the Lees. His Godparents were George and Martha Washington. Dennis and Elenor's gratitude to Ferdinando Fairfax probably led them to name one of their sons Ferdinand.

Ferdinando Fairfax (1769-1820)

Born at Towlston, the Fairfax County plantation of his parents, he spent a large part of his life in Jefferson County, Virginia (now West Virginia), serving as Justice of the Peace and buying land. He moved to Alexandria in 1810. He engaged in a variety of large-scale business enterprises, most of them unsuccessful. In 1790 he published his "Plan for Liberating the Negroes within the United States," which advocated gradual emancipation and passage of a congressional act to offer inducements for owners to free their enslaved and assume the expense of colonizing freed people in Africa. He freed several of his own enslaved, including Dennis Berry, and sold others with the understanding that they be freed in the future.

Ferdinando Fairfax
(1766-1820)
Public Domain

The story of Dennis and Elenor's life was recounted by George O. Seilhamer, a well-known local historian, in the "Public Weekly Opinion," a Chambersburg, Pennsylvania newspaper. In his article of 4 June 1897, he told of Chambersburg right before the battle of Gettysburg when the local black community took flight as Confederate troops moved northward.   Seilhamer claimed that General Robert E. Lee sought out the Berry house on his way to Gettysburg "to pay a visit of courtesy." The Berry family had already fled. The historian explained that "among the slaves of Henry Lee at the time of the birth of his son, Robert Edward, was a bright mulatto girl who became the nurse of the infant Robert." Seilhamer said that Dennis Berry, (who had been manumitted by Ferdinando Fairfax), wanted this girl to become his wife "and worked diligently for the means to buy her from her distinguished master." Seilhamer explained that Henry Lee was in debtor's prison and did not have the means to free Elenor himself.   An obituary of a George Bell in a 22 July 1873 Chambersburg newspaper reveals exactly when the Berry family went to Chambersburg. Mr. Bell said that his family moved from Fairfax County Virginia to Chambersburg "in company with Dennis Berry and other families" in 1814. He remembered this date clearly because they arrived "in the evening, when all the town was jubilant over the news just received of peace having been declared between the United States and Great Britain, in the year 1814." A Chambersburg legal document shows that in April 1814 Dennis Berry ("Blackman") bought a house in Chambersburg, probably at what is now #425 South Main Street (formerly Front Street).

If the above events are correct, Elenor probably was never enslaved at Sully but probably belonged to the Richard Bland Lee family when they lived in Alexandria. The Federal Census of 1820 and 1830 shows the Berry family living in Chambersburg, all "Free Colored Persons" (see box below for a notable event in Dennis' life). In Pennsylvania's Septennial Census in 1835, Dennis Berry is listed as a "labourer" and "Coloured." Only heads of household were included. A Franklin County probate record listing an inventory of Dennis Berry's estate states that he died on 3 December 1836. In the 1840 Census, "Ellen Berry" alone is in the census with seven other people. In the 1850 Census, Elenor Berry is alone again in Chambersburg with her children and grandchildren.

Can her descendants be found? A day spent at the Chambersburg Historical Society yielded old phone books, obituaries, newspaper articles and census information that allowed a match of the Berry family with a family tree located on Ancestry.com's web site. The person who posted it knew little of her family in Chambersburg but included a death certificate that linked her grandfather with a great-great grandchild of Elenor's. Elenor, therefore, was her fifth great-grandmother. Contacted through Ancestry.com, she acknowledged that her grandmother, a Berry, had moved to Maryland decades ago and lost contact with any Berry's that still lived in Chambersburg. Below is the genealogical path from Elenor to the young woman found through her family tree posted on Ancestry.com.

Descendants of Elenor and Dennis Berry
Elenor Berry (1784-1875) Dennis Berry (1790-1836)
Ferdinand I (1824-1900)
Ferdinand II (1856-1933)
One of Ferdinand's 11 children, Arthur Scott Berry (1878-1925)
Arthur's son, Preston Leroy Berry (1907-1960)
Preston's daughter, Emma Jane Berry (1928-2011)
Emma's daughter (still living)
Emma's granddaughter (still living)

Dennis Berry Attends First Annual Convention of the People of Color

William Lloyd Garrison's newspaper, "The Liberator," reported that the First Annual Convention of the People of Color was held in June 1831 in Philadelphia and that Dennis Berry, from Chambersburg, attended and was elected to a committee to discuss the opening of a college for black men in New Haven, CT, the first of its kind. The vision was to make it a collaborative effort with Yale College (later Yale University). The Mayor of New Haven called a town meeting immediately to vote on a resolution opposing the "Negro College." A committee composed of a "who's who" of Yale leaders and New Haven's political elite claimed that the existence of a "Negro college" would harm Yale College and the other area schools, the Negro college being "incompatible with the prosperity, if not the existence of the present institutions of learning, and will be destructive of the best interests of the city." After the failure to get buy-in by Yale College and the community, it took more than 20 years before efforts to found a black college in the United States succeeded—Wilberforce College in Ohio.

Elliot

Richard Bland Lee wrote a letter to his brother-in-law Zaccheus Collins (1764-1831) in March 1802 offering to give him an enslaved child named Elliot: "Elliot, the son of Patty whom you took a fancy to…I will send him begging you to accept him as a token of my regard. He will be six years old in the coming summer." No subsequent letters from the Lees or Collins confirm that Elliot actually went to Zaccheus' home in Philadelphia. However, the Federal Censuses for 1800, 1810, 1820 and 1830 appear to confirm it. The 1800 Census, before Elliot would have arrived, counts "0 free colored persons" in the Collins household. In the 1810 Census, the first one that would note Elliot's presence, the count is 3 "white persons" and the "number of all other free persons" as 1. Zaccheus Collins apparently gave Elliot his freedom before the state law required it. Section Four of the 1780 Pennsylvania Law stated that every "negro or mulatto child" born of enslaved mothers after the bill's passage would be considered "servants" to their masters until they turned 28, when they would receive their freedom. The 1820 Census of the Collins household includes "1 free colored male age 26-44" and the 1830 census includes "1 free colored male age 36-54." These ages in the Census conform with Elliot's birth date. Further confirmation that Elliot went to live with Zaccheus Collins is that Patty (his mother) was mentioned in the 1809 indenture document that listed the enslaved people belonging to Richard Bland Lee, but Elliot was not listed (he was born around 1796).

How did Elliot fit into the Collins family? He probably received a decent education because Quakers believed that this was important; Elizabeth Collins Lee was unusual, for her time and place, in educating at least two of her enslaved females. Elliot could have been used in the family business, particularly since Zaccheus had no sons. Zaccheus and his father Stephen were wealthy merchants in Philadelphia who procured many items, both domestic and foreign, for Sully. Elliot could also have been used to help with Zaccheus' avocation as a botanist and plant collector. A plant species was named after Zaccheus, and after his death, his herbarium became part of a collection at the Academy of Natural Sciences of Philadelphia.

Zaccheus Collins died in 1831, and his wife pre-deceased him so there are no more Federal Census records for this family. Collins died intestate (without a will), thereby leaving no bequest that might have named Elliot. An important unknown is what last name Elliot adopted. Enslaved sometimes took the names of their owners but more often took other names that were meaningful to them in some way (see box below). There is no "colored person" named Elliot Lee or Elliot Collins born around 1796 in Virginia and living in Pennsylvania or any other state in either the Federal Census of 1840 or 1850. He could have died, taken another name, or moved westward, as did so many Americans.

Names Adopted by Those Formerly Enslaved

According to Herbert G. Gutman, the author of "The Black Family in Slavery & Freedom, 1750-1925," almost all enslaved people had a second name unknown to their white masters and generally different than the names of their owners. When freed, they did not take the last name of their owners but instead used the surname they had always used but kept hidden. For example, none of George Washington's enslaved took the name Washington. Over thirty former enslaved people or their children formerly owned by Robert Carter of Nomini Hall were registered as free blacks in Fairfax County; none of these are named Carter. The pattern seems too pervasive to be coincidental. The only enslaved people owned by Richard Bland Lee known to have taken his name were Samuel and Barbara Lee, plaintiffs in a lawsuit discussed above. These enslaved people sued Elizabeth Collins Lee for their freedom and might have been given the Lee name for legal reasons. This typical naming convention makes even more difficult the task of finding the enslaved after their freedom and their descendants.

Ludwell

In 1804, Ludwell, one of Sully's enslaved, escaped. Elizabeth Collins Lee appeared incensed and said to her brother in a letter, "Mr. Lee has been much perplex'd to find Ludwell--who absconded with all of Mr. Lee's valuable tools…a true proof of the ingratitude of Slavery--too much indulged and his freedom promised in 6 years…" With the help of Elizabeth's brother in Philadelphia, Ludwell was returned.

We next find Ludwell in the 1809 indenture document listed as "Ludwell, and his wife Nancy, and their children Caroline, Harriet, Frederick, Ludwell, and Barbara." A February 1817 document in Sully's library claims that Elizabeth Lee "freed slave Beaver Ludwell and Nancy, his wife, under the condition that slave agrees to keep wife." [note this document was written after the Lees moved to the District]

A document in the District's Deed Book #21 of 10 November 1851 suggests that Ludwell must not have agreed to the caveat Elizabeth Lee imposed because Nancy and her family were still in servitude at that time. The purpose of the document was to allow Elizabeth to give five enslaved people to her son, Richard B. Lee II, to be held in trust for her daughter, Cornelia Macrae. They were Nancy and her four children Frederick, Caroline, Amy, and Mary. Where was Ludwell, Nancy's husband? Did he escape again or perhaps he had died?

Elizabeth Collins' will of 1858 freed only Caroline in the Ludwell family: "and in consideration of the good conduct and fidelity of my negro man, Frank Madison, and my woman Caroline, my only remaining slaves, I hereby emancipate them, and recommend them to the care and protection of my children."

"The District of Columbia Free Negro Registers, 1821-1861" does not include any of the Ludwell family. The Federal Census for 1860 and for 1870 show no one with the last name Ludwell and first name Caroline. The Federal Census for 1870, the first after emancipation, shows no one with the last name Ludwell and first name matching the names of Nancy or her children. The Slavery Schedules for 1850 and 1860 are not detailed enough to know if some or all of the Ludwell family joined the Macraes' enslaved. The Slavery Schedule for 1850 shows that Dr. Macrae was a large slave owner in Prince William County, Virginia, owning 23 enslaved people in that year, ranging from a 1-year old male to a 90-year-old female. The Slavery Schedule for 1860 shows Dr. Macrae owning 15 slaves, ranging from a 4-year old male to a 42-year old male. Only the names of the slave owners are given in these schedules.

Some good evidence exists for what happened to Ludwell's daughter Harriet, who was in the 1809 indenture document but was not mentioned in Elizabeth Collins' 1858 will that freed her sister Caroline. Harriet probably married a freed slave named Robert Gunnell. Elizabeth Collins Lee's will gave to her son Zaccheus Collins Lee "one small tenement of land…in Fairfax County…at this time occupied by negro, Robert Gunnell and Harriet, her children and grand-children, the slaves of Major R.B. Lee." Major Lee was Elizabeth's oldest son. A 1990 book entitled "On the Fringe of Fame" by Elizabeth Fleming Rhodes, a descendant of Major Lee, reports that a letter from Elizabeth to son Richard reveals that Richard Bland Lee had given Harriet and her children to Major Lee, date unspecified. She said, "How dearly and fully you paid for the gift your Father made to you of Harriot (her spelling) and her children, a curse on you rather than present." We do not know the reason for this sour judgment, but Richard Bland Lee was sued posthumously in 1834 for failing to repay a debt and unlawfully divesting himself of some of his enslaved people who were to be used as collateral (discussed above), Harriet being one of those enslaved. Probably in the eyes of the bank, such a "gift" was not legal.

Harriet's husband, Robert Gunnell, probably had been enslaved in Fairfax County by a slave owner named Robert Gunnell, who freed all of his enslaved people when he died in 1828, declaring "…my will and particular desire is that all my negroes be free I say free they and all their increase forever." Some of the names of those enslaved and their physical descriptions are found in Fairfax County's Register of Freed Slaves, but Robert Gunnell is not among them. Sometimes these entries were only numbers and not names. Harriet does not appear in the Register as a freed slave of either

Major R.B. Lee or his father, and we know from a recently discovered document that she was not freed until the District of Columbia freed its slaves in April 1862, nine months before the Emancipation Proclamation.   That newly discovered source is a legal document signed by Ann Matilda Lee Washington (one of Richard Bland Lee's daughters) in April 1862 acknowledging the freedom of Ludwell Gunnell, Harriet's son. If Harriet had been freed before that, her son would have been freed also because the law specified that children followed the status of their mother, not their father. By signing the document that freed Ludwell, Ann Matilda was eligible for the $300 that the government paid in compensation to former slave owners who were loyal to the Union. Ann Matilda declared that she "bears true and faithful allegiance to the Government of the United States, and that she has not borne arms against the United States in the present rebellion, nor in any way given aid or comfort thereto." Ludwell Gunnell was said to be five foot eight inches and "a good dining room and house servant, likely and strong…"

Robert and Harriet Gunnell appear in the Federal Census for Fairfax County for 1850, 1870 and 1880, and Harriet's death in 1883 at the age of 83 is recorded in the Virginia Deaths and Burials Index, 1853-1917.   Their marriage was registered in the District of Columbia in 1866. We do not know if they were "married" earlier in an informal or religious ceremony.

Using records in Ancestry.com's data base allows the partial construction of Robert and Harriet's family tree down to the present generation. Only one line—the Ashton line—is currently traceable to a descendant living today.

Ludwell and Nancy
Their Daughter Harriet (1795-1883); husband Robert Gunnell (b. 1795)
Their Daughter Sarah Gunnel (b. 1834); husband William Ashton (b. 1830)
Their Son Ludwell Ashton (b. 1869)
Ludwell's Son Kellogg B. Ashton (1898-1984)
Kellogg's Daughter Leonora (1926-2017)
Leonora's Daughter Linda (1961-living)

Isaac

In October 1791, a Loudoun County court document recorded the sale of "one negroe boy named Isaac about four years" by Richard Bland Lee to "George Shiveley for the price of one shilling." Loudoun County Land Tax Records of 1788 show that some of Sully's land was farmed by four tenant farmers, one of whom was George Shiveley, and Title tables list him in 1785 as overseer. While Lee was away serving in Congress, he referred to Shiveley as such in letters to his brother Theodorick: "I hope…you will stimulate Shivelly to exert himself in collecting as many of my debts as possible during the winter…" George's brother Jacob also worked at Sully, but with lesser responsibilities. The Federal Census of 1810 shows one enslaved owned by George Shively, which is probably Isaac. Born in 1787, Isaac would have been 23 years old. George and his wife joined the local Baptist church known as Frying Pan Meeting House (see box below), and in 1814 the church minutes indicate that the church baptized "a Black man belonging to George Shivily," likely Isaac. [Note: The name Shiveley is spelled various ways in official documents, which have been preserved here. It is not clear which spelling is correct.]

According to an article on "Sully's Shively Brothers" by Fairfax County historian, Debbie Robison, George decided that his future was in Indiana but while traveling through Ohio in 1815 near the present town of Kingston, he contracted a fatal illness and died. The task of providing for the family fell on George's 18-year old son Jacob. The family abandoned its plans to press on to Indiana, floating back down the Scioto River and settling in Ohio on Paint Creek. Jacob hauled salt and whiskey to and from Zanesville for a while and then bought land for farming and stock-raising, according to a 1902 history of Ross County, Ohio.

No mention is made of Isaac in this trek west. Ohio abolished slavery in 1802, and Indiana abolished it in 1816. The Federal Census of 1820 shows no "free colored person" living with George's son Jacob. In the most likely scenario, Isaac had gone his own way by that time since he would have been a free man in the states through which the Shively family travelled. The Federal Census data for Indiana and Ohio record many black families with the name Shively. There are no family trees yet available in Ancestry.com that link any of them with Sully's Isaac.

Frying Pan Meeting House

A Virginia historic marker notes that Frying Pan Meeting House was constructed by 1791 on land donated by the Carter family and was used for Baptist services until 1968.   The property was conveyed to the Fairfax County Park Authority in 1984. According to church minutes, available online, by 1840 the congregation consisted of 33 whites and 29 blacks. Both black and white members are buried in the church cemetery, but the graves are segregated and no names of black members remain on the gravestones. Enslaved people were welcome to join but were segregated from the rest of the congregation in life as well as in death. They worshipped from the galleries that lined both sides of the building. In 1833, the church appointed a Black man named Jupiter "to try to keep order among the coloured people in the gallery in times of worship."   In the church records, the enslaved black members were referred to as "belonging to…" or "the property of…"

None of Sully's enslaved are mentioned by name in the church minutes (see previous section on Isaac) despite being the closest church to Sully. Neither of the Lees, in their voluminous correspondence, ever mentioned their enslaved people attending church. It is not until the Haights and Barlows moved to Sully in the early 1840s that their enslaved/servants are mentioned in letters as attending Frying Pan Meeting House. In an 1844 letter written by Amy Haight, she reports that Ester and Jim "went to Frying pan to Church last first day"(meaning the first Sunday of the month).

Henrietta Rains

An obituary of 20 August 1876 in the Van Buren Press of Crawford County, Arkansas, reported the death of Henrietta Rains. It said that she was born in 1769 and belonged to Richard Bland Lee of Virginia: "She remembered well when congress met in Philadelphia, and often saw George Washington. At the burning of Washington City [during the War of 1812], she was living in that city." She had five living children at that time. According to her, she was sold to Gen. Gabriel James Rains of the US Army after the death of Richard Bland Lee. She was subsequently sold to the DuVall family until after the Civil War when she was given her freedom. The obituary notes that "she was noted for her clear memory of events which had transpired during her long life…and in her conversation and manners showed the refinement brought by having been associated with the most cultivated families."

Henrietta may have been the "Henny and her child Eleanor" in the 1809 indenture document that listed those enslaved at Sully. Henny is a nickname for Henrietta. She would have been 30 years old at the time. The fact that she remembered when the Congress met in Philadelphia would have encompassed the years that the Lees were at Sully. Congress met in Philadelphia, but not successively, from 1774-1783 and again in 1790-1800. The Lees moved to the District some time in 1815 so Henrietta may well have witnessed the burning of bridges during the War of 1812 as the war lasted until 1815.

Henrietta claimed that after Richard Bland Lee's death in 1827, she became the property of General Gabriel James Rains, "attending him through all of his campaigns." Exactly how this happened is unknown, but we do know that both Richard Bland Lee II and Rains were graduates of West Point and served together later in the Seminole War (1835-42). After his father's death, Richard had requested several furloughs to attend to his father's "much embarrassed and unsettled affairs," (from the aforementioned book, "On the Fringe of Fame") and it might have been at this time while Rains was also in the capital area that Richard saw an opportunity to sell one of his father's enslaved. It is unknown where or how Henrietta "accompanied" Rains during his military career, but they both ended up in Arkansas, perhaps because of the strategic location of Fort Smith. A large military presence was established there during the 1830s when Indian tribes from the American Southeast were moved west of the Mississippi River. Fort Smith was also used as a base during the Mexican War (1866-48), in which General Rains served. The 1860 Slave Schedule for Van Buren City shows that Major. G. J. Rains owned 6 slaves, one of whom was a 70-year old black female, probably Henrietta. On the same schedule appears a James A. DuVall, with 11 slaves, probably the same slave owner who later bought Henrietta from Rains.

No trace can be found of Henrietta's five children. It is not likely that they were also bought by Rains and accompanied him on his military ramblings. The Crawford County Genealogical Society stated in an e-mail to me that they had never heard of any Blacks by the name of Rains in the area but posted requests for help on their website. They said that some DuVall descendants remain in Crawford County.

General Gabriel James Rains
(1803-1881)
Library of Congress

Milly/Milley

In 1809, Richard Bland Lee sold one enslaved female named Milly "with her increase" to John P. Van Ness of the District of Columbia. "With her increase" meant that any children that Milly had in the future would also belong to Van Ness. In Richard Bland Lee's 1809 indenture document, Milly is listed as a daughter of John and his wife Alice. Van Ness served as a US Representative from New York from 1801 to 1803 and was then appointed as a major in the District of Columbia militia. He was promoted to major general in 1813, serving as the Commanding General of the District of Columbia National Guard during the War of 1812. He was the mayor of Washington D.C. from 1830 to 1834. He died in 1846 and was entombed in the Van Ness Mausoleum at his residence, which was later transferred to Oak Hill Cemetery in Georgetown.

John Peter Van Ness
(1769-1846)
Library of Congress

According to the Federal Census of 1820, Van Ness owned 12 "slaves". Milly was probably his one female slave, age 14-25, perhaps being the mother of one or two of the 5 male slaves under 14. The estate files of Van Ness (Van Ness-Philip Family Papers) in the library of the New York Historical Society reveal that Van Ness sold "Milley" in March 1827 to Benjamin Lewis of Maury County, Tennessee, "to serve on his sister Mrs. Hardin" of the same County. Lewis bought her for $300, and the sales document stipulated that after 20 years, Milley would be given her freedom.

However, her (cursive is hard to read but it could say "sons") and her increase (her future children) would remain "slaves for life."

We could find no records that shed light on who Benjamin and his sister were other than residents of Tennessee. John H. Eaton was appointed by Van Ness to oversee Milley's contract. He was US Senator from Tennessee from 1818 to 1829. As Chairman of the Senate Committee on the District of Columbia, he probably knew Van Ness well, but it is unclear why he would have helped Benjamin Lewis buy Milley. We found no records for Milley after she was freed in March 1847, but we do not know what last name she chose after freedom.

Registers of Enslaved who were Freed

In 1793 the Virginia General Assembly passed a law requiring "every free negro or mulatto" to register annually with the clerk of the court of the city or county. A copy was given to them certifying their free status, allowing them to travel about and accept work. Such registration also was required in the District of Columbia and some Maryland counties. According to the introductory notes to the Fairfax County Register, a substantial majority of those registered were free by birth. If not freeborn, the majority of the remaining were freed by last will and testament. The third way to achieve freedom was by a deed filed in the county court, which simply freed a man, woman, or their offspring, for all future time. Frequently a token payment, such as "one dollar to me in hand paid" was cited in the deed. The deeds are recorded in the land books, a reminder of the slaves' status as property under the law.

Although a wealth of information can be found from this source, it cannot be assumed that all those who were enslaved and later freed were so recorded. The introduction to the Fairfax County Register, added in recent times, notes that "preliminary analysis of the registers indicates that the laws requiring registration of free blacks were enforced with some degree of laxity." The law requiring all those who were freed after 1806 to leave Virginia also went largely unenforced, according to this source. Moreover, some registry books are missing.

Samuel and Barbara Lee

As detailed above in Chapter 1, the enslaved Samuel and Barbara Lee, belonging to Richard Bland Lee before his death in 1827, contended in a court case in 1834 that they should be freed because they were taken unlawfully from Sully to live in Alexandria for a short time and then to the home of Elizabeth Collins Lee in the District of Columbia. The Federal Census for 1830 shows no entry for Elizabeth Lee as head of household so there is no proof that the enslaved were living with her before the court case. Because Samuel and Barbara did not win their court case, it would be useful to know if the Federal Census of 1840 showed that they were living with Elizabeth six years after the court ruling. While the Federal Census for that year shows no entry for Elizabeth Lee as the head of household, she most likely was the "free white female 60-69" who was living with her daughter Ann Matilda and her husband Dr. Bailey Washington in the District of Columbia. He owned seven enslaved people, none of whom would fit the description of Samuel, but Barbara could fit the description of one of the family's five enslaved females. The 1850 Federal Census shows Elizabeth Lee still living (by name) with her daughter's family, but no enslaved people were living with them.

Lee is a very common name, and it is almost impossible to identify these enslaved after their freedom, but there is one intriguing entry in the Federal Census of 1850. A Samuel Lee, age 65 and a blacksmith (fits the description of Samuel in the 1809 indenture document), was a mulatto living in the District of Columbia with his family. He and his wife were born in Virginia but all seven of their children were born in the District. The oldest son was named Richard. If this is Sully's Samuel, it would mean that he was given his freedom. The manumissions book for the District of Columbia, 1821-1861, does not include a Samuel or a Barbara Lee, but there are many reasons why their names might not have been listed (see box above).

Chapter 3: Enslaved People of Sully's Owners from 1811 to 1842

These years were the most turbulent for the farm and its enslaved. A succession of owners and a cavalier attitude to those bought and sold, their whereabouts only occasionally recorded, added to the inherent insecurity of their lives. Robert S. Gamble's book, "Sully: The Biography of a House" helped untangle this complex chapter in Sully's history, which built on local historian Louise Ryder's discoveries about later owners Robertson and Swartwout.

At the beginning of this period, the new owner of Sully was Francis Lightfoot Lee, who appeared a good fit. He was a Lee cousin and the son of Richard Henry Lee, a signer of the Declaration of Independence. A bright and resourceful gentleman farmer, he relied heavily on tenants and hired laborers to work the farm, but also the enslaved--domestic servants as well as field hands--while hiring some from his brother-in-law, William Maffitt. A "Slaves Wanted" ad in the Alexandria Gazette of 20 February 1811 announced that "eight or ten Virginia slaves, boys, women and men, of good character" were wanted for "a liberal price in cash" by Francis L. Lee of Sully. The personal property tax of 1817 indicated that there were 23 people enslaved at Sully. The only one identified by name during that time was "a negro girl named Lucy, 12 or 13 years old, 5 feet high, of middling stature…not a dark black, having a round full face with rather high cheekbones, from Maryland." This information was on a "certificate of importation of slave into Commonwealth" of May 1811 that noted she had been "acquired by marriage."

In 1816, Lee's world began to spiral downward. His second wife died in childbirth, leaving him with a newborn and four small children. Three months after his wife's death, in October 1816, Lee advertised the sale of Sully in the Alexandria Gazette. A sale never took place, and Lee continued to live at Sully for almost ten years more with some of his children. In 1820, Lee suffered a nervous collapse from which he never recovered. In May of that year, the Chancery Court of Fairfax County appointed Lee's nephew, Richard Henry Lee II, as head of the Administrative Committee to "take care of the estate…for the safekeeping and good management thereof." According to a Lee vs. Lee Lawyers Brief (Chancery Causes #59-205) of May 1820, the farm yielded $1500-2000 per annum net profit and included "from fifteen to twenty negroes." The only enslaved people named in a document was in 1825 when it was noted that "negro Phil and family" were sold for $700. In 1825 Francis Lee was taken to the Pennsylvania Hospital in Philadelphia and afterward put in the care of a Quaker couple in Bucks County. Late in life he was brought back to Virginia to live with his children and died in 1850.

Richard Henry Lee II's appointment as Sully administrator was unfortunate. He was incompetent and the dishonesty of his overseers exacerbated the problems. Over a decade later, he would be sued by his uncle's heirs and charged with neglect and mismanagement. He was asked to render a full accounting of income and disbursements and to specify "those blacks who had been sold." After Richard Henry Lee II's failure, he was replaced with Colonel W.C.B. Butler in 1827, who was removed by the county court in 1830 for incompetence and replaced with Colonel George Washington Hunter, only to be replaced in 1834 with Henry Tazewell Harrison, a Lee relative. An 1830 document filed with the County (Historic Records Center of the Fairfax Circuit Court; Fairfax County Will Index 1742-1936) appears to be an inventory and list of those enslaved at Sully completed "at the request of Col. Geo. W. Hunter." The list is presented here exactly as given. It was said to be complete except for "the young negros born since."

Negro Jacob	62 years and diseased
Mosses	29
Willoughby	37
Dennis	35
James	32
Clement	42
Clara	28
Frankly	31
Dick	11 very sickly with the disentary
Charles	7 Ill with the same complaint
Edwin	5
Tom	11 Killed by wagon & team before this inventory returned to Court
William	3
Susan	1
Cyrus	1

The sad story of Sully's deterioration can be read online; see Fairfax Chancery Case Lee vs. Lee at www.lva.virginia.gov/chancery/case_detail.asp?CFN=059-1830-004.

This period of time was not only one of personal misfortune for the Francis Lightfoot Lee family and Sully's enslaved but also one of depressed economic conditions for Northern Virginia, caused by changes in the viability of its major cash crop, tobacco, and the pull of settlers westward where land was cheaper. Official population counts at the time show that the population of Virginia actually decreased by two percent from 1830 to 1840, and between 1790 and 1830, the white population of Fairfax County declined from 7,611 to 4,892.

Converging Economic Factors Affect Slavery in Northern Virginia

During the time that Francis Lightfoot Lee owned Sully, the days of tobacco as a monoculture in Northern Virginia had almost disappeared. Growing tobacco had depleted the nutrients in the soil; old fields had to be left fallow for one-two decades to recover. Growing tobacco was also highly labor-intensive. Millions of seedlings had to be replanted from seed beds to the fields and constantly weeded, pruned, and picked free of the dreaded horn worm.   The supply of new enslaved labor began to dry up. Congress passed a bill in 1809 that prohibited "the import of slaves into any US port" although it allowed inter-state sales to continue. The last converging factor was the invention of the cotton gin in 1793, which for the first time allowed the mechanized processing of short-staple cotton that was grown in the Deep South.

All of these factors resulted in increased demand for slaves in the Deep South and a "surplus" in Virginia, resulting in a clamor to ship them southward. Alexandria became a chief center of this lucrative trade, and the local firm Franklin and Armfield became the largest slave trading brokerage in the country. Its building has now been converted into the Freedom House Museum. Visitors can see holding pens where, it is estimated, as many as a million people passed through between 1828 and 1860 on their way to bondage in Mississippi and Louisiana.

The children of Francis Lightfoot Lee finally decided that Sully was unprofitable and should be sold and that the remaining enslaved should be sold in the Deep South. Sully's administrator wrote to the farm manager in 1835: "You will please bear in mind the southern expedition and see if it will be possible to get any or all of those negroes off." Those enslaved probably traveled from

Virginia to Louisiana and Mississippi in "coffle gangs" (chain gangs such as the one pictured below).

Coffle Gang
Library of Congress

In 1836, an Englishman, John Robertson, bought the farm for only half the price that Francis Lee paid, and he only paid half the asking price up front. The season's crops were included as well as an enslaved family—Dennis, Clara and their small son (Dennis and Clara were listed in the above 1930 inventory). The fact that none of the other enslaved in the inventory were mentioned in the bill of sale probably means that all of them had indeed been sold South. Robertson left Sully in 1837 to return to England, ostensibly for business reasons, but in 1838, he was arrested for forgery there. The administrator of the estate, Henry Harrison, sent a messenger to Sully to tell the enslaved family to "immediately pack up their all and come to me." Harrison secured an injunction restraining Robertson's wife from selling any of Sully's assets, but she had already disposed of some things. Before Robertson left, he had taken Clara's son to Alexandria and possibly sold the child. Harrison wanted Lee, the former administrator, to "immediately find out where the boy is and to serve a notice that the boy is not the property of Robertson and warning against any disposition of him." In 1837, Robertson (or Drake, his real name) was convicted, sent to prison for two years and then transported for life to Botany Bay, Australia, according to the Home Office Criminal Register, County of Lancaster, England. Harrison filed suit to repossess the farm. In the spring of 1838, the Fairfax County Court returned Sully to the Lees and authorized another sale of the estate at public auction. Nothing more was recorded about the fate of the enslaved family.

The next owner of Sully was William Swartwout, a native New Yorker and a speculator in slaves and commodities in the Deep South. In his book on Sully, Robert Gamble opines that Swartwout probably arranged for the sale south of Sully's enslaved as he was friendly with business associates and relatives of the Lees. In 1838, Swartwout made an offer for Sully and in October 1839, he returned to take possession, having to rout Robertson's wife from the property. He returned to Mississippi and left Thomas N. Stewart in charge, telling Stewart, "I have bought the negro man that lived at Sully called Jim. I shall bring him with me as he is very anxious to get back again." He did in fact bring back Jim, according to Arthur Lee, Francis Lightfoot Lee's son. The 1840 Census (schedules for Fairfax County) indicates that Swartwout kept 13 slaves there, eight of whom were listed as agricultural laborers. An economic recession, which soured the booming economy in the south, and Swartwout's declining health left the Lees to wonder if they would ever get paid the full amount for Sully (they had only received half). In 1841 Swartwout died intestate and his possessions sold. Fairfax County will books list personal possessions including two pairs of socks, a gold watch and two toothbrushes, the season's yield of corn and hay, and the stock and farming implements, but no enslaved were mentioned.

This period in Sully's life was so chaotic that none of the descendants of these enslaved could be traced. Few were left on the farm in Virginia, and none that had been transported South were ever heard of again.

Chapter 4: Enslaved People of the Haights and Barlows and Their Descendants

In January 1842 Sully was again up for sale along with one negro man, perhaps the Jim previously owned by Swartwout. It was bought in September by Jacob and Amy Haight from Dutchess County, New York. Later, their daughter and son-in-law, James and Maria Barlow, joined them. They were industrious and progressive farmers. They rented some enslaved labor from their neighbors but they also owned several enslaved people despite their Quaker background. The 1850 Slave Schedule attached to the Federal Census shows that Jacob Haight owned five enslaved: one male black age 30, one male black age 22, one female black age 21, one male black age 19 and one female mulatto age 4. His son Alexander owned two in the 1860 Slave Schedule: one male black age 35 and one female mulatto age 14.

Unlike the Lee family who rarely mentioned their enslaved by name in correspondence, the Haights and Barlows often talked of their enslaved, almost like family.

- In an 1844 letter from Amy Haight to the Barlows in New York before they permanently moved to Virginia, she writes, "I red a part of thy last letter to Ester. Shee said don't forget to remember my love to Miss Maria when you right agane. Shee and Jim went to frying pan to Church Last first day. She has a fine little darkey…Fenton often asks me when I have heard from Miss Maria and…when she is a coming home."
- In a 6 January 1846 letter to her parents, Maria Barlow says, "Last Thursday was the usual hiring day did you keep Esther and little Phil…"
- In a letter from Phebe and Amy Haight to Maria Barlow on 26 January 1846, she replies to the above question: "Thomas has hired her for this year…we shall not have but one black on the place in a short time, Thomas's are here at present, they are repairing the house he intends moving in…."

Jim in the correspondence above is probably the enslaved man who was included in the sale of Sully to the Haights in 1842, and perhaps he was the black male age 30 in the 1850 Census. Neither he nor Ester appears in the 1860 Slave Schedule, and we have no information about their subsequent life. Ester, in fact, might have been an enslaved who was hired out. A common practice in the area was for a farmer to hire enslaved workers from neighbors. The employer provided food, clothing, shelter and medical care, in addition to the wage paid to the slave owner. Annual contracts ran for fifty-one weeks, and communities set aside one day at the beginning of each year as "hiring days"—in the Cub Run area, the date was January first. This corresponds with the 6 January 1846 letter cited above, the Haights referring to "Last Thursday" as the usual hiring day and saying that "Thomas has hired her for this year…"

Fenton and the Lucas Family

In 1844 Amy Haight wrote to her daughter, as mentioned above, that "Fenton often asks me when I have heard from Miss Maria…" It is probable that Fenton was enslaved at Sully at the time. The 1850 Federal Census Slave Schedule for Amy's husband, Jacob Haight, listed three enslaved adult men, ages, 30, 22 and 19. It is likely that Jim, mentioned in the section above, was the 30-year old, leaving Fenton to be 22 or 19 (born in 1828 or 1831). A 1931 Death Certificate for Fenton Lucas, born in Stafford County, Virginia, and dying in Dranesville, Fairfax County, Virginia, gives his age as 103, meaning that he would have been born in 1828.

In 1891, one of Jacob and Amy Haight's grandsons, Stephen Sweet Haight, married Henrietta Lucas, "a mulatto," in the District of Columbia. Henrietta's father was named Fenton R. Lucas. His marriage record shows that he was born in 1845. Given that "Fenton" is an unusual given name and because it is common that names are passed through families, we judge that these Fentons were in the same family, but we are not sure of their relationship. Henrietta's father's marriage record reported that his father's name was John so it appears that the older Fenton was not his father. The elder Fenton and John could have been brothers. The Lucas family's ties to Sully probably explain how Stephen Sweet-Haight became acquainted with Henrietta Lucas. A Haight descendant reported to me that when they married, Stephen Sweet-Haight was disowned by his family. Stephen and Henrietta later divorced. The Lucas/Haight family tree known from official documents and family records is:

Fenton Lucas (b. 1841/45) married Ann Pierce/Thornton. The names of her father and mother were given as Samuel and Matilda Pierce/Thornton. We do not know why two last names appear in the official documents.

Daughter Henrietta Lucas (1873-1943) married Stephen Sweet-Haight
Their Son Floyd Sweet Haight (1886-1957)
Floyd's Daughter Dorothy E. (1922-living)
Dorothy's Daughter Deloris (1938-living)
Deloris' Son Ernest (1969-living)

Enslaved members of the Lucas family were numerous in Fairfax and Loudoun Counties in the early 1800s, but it is unclear how they were all related. In 1829 nine of them emigrated with a group of 58 emancipated slaves to Liberia, a journey sponsored by the Loudoun Manumission and Emigration Society (see box below). Two of them, Mars and Jesse Lucas, wrote back to the family of their former slave owners to tell them about life in their new country and to get news about their families. The Loudoun County Museum owns the originals (see Lucas-Heaton papers at www.loudounmuseum.org/exhibits). The collection is a poignant look at their travails—death of children and wives, difficulty earning a living, and even an attack by the natives.

The American Colonization Society

The Society for the Colonization of Free People of Color of America, commonly known as the American Colonization Society (ACS), was founded in 1816 to encourage and support the voluntary migration of free African-Americans to the continent of Africa. Interestingly, Richard Bland Lee and Bushrod Washington, one of Lee's creditors and the nephew of George Washington, were two of its early organizers. The ACS was supported by two usually opposing groups—slaveholders, who believed that repatriation was a way to remove free blacks and avoid slave rebellions, and a coalition of evangelicals, philanthropists and abolitionists who wanted slaves to be free but believed blacks would face better chances for freedom in Africa than in America where they were generally not welcome in the South or North. From the beginning, the majority of black Americans regarded the ACS with disdain.

Late into his first term as president, Lincoln publicly abandoned the idea of colonization, reportedly after speaking about it with Frederick Douglass. Colonizing proved expensive, and Congress refused to fund emigration. Only a few thousand free blacks were transported.

Another tie of the Lucas family to Sully might be through the marriage of Fenton Lucas and Ann Pierce/Thornton. In the 1809 indenture document drawn up for Richard Bland Lee, detailed above, one of his listed slaves was Thornton (a cook). We know nothing more about him. The 1867

Loudoun County document, registering the marriage of Ann and Fenton Lucas, asks "By Whom Age Approved," and the answer is "Henry Thornton, negro." Henry might have been the brother of Ann's mother Matilda. The minutes of Frying Pan Meeting House in the 1870s lists Henry Thornton and Sanford Thornton as "coloured" members, indicating that they lived in the Sully area. It is possible that Henry, Sanford and Matilda Thornton were siblings and that all were descendants of Thornton the cook.

In 2003, the descendants of Stephen Sweet-Haight and Henrietta Lucas gathered at Sully for a family reunion. This photo was supplied for use in this book by Dorothy's daughter Deloris.

Cleo

Phebe Haight (Alexander's wife and daughter-in-law of Jacob and Amy Haight) owned one enslaved female named Cleo, according to Haight family records, now in the Fairfax County Public Library, and interviews in the 1970s with descendant Alexander L. Haight. Alexander Haight said in 1971 that "Cleo was a young girl when my father was a baby. She was hired at Sully plantation to take care of my father. She was about sixteen years old. It wasn't long until the war broke out. In the first year of the war she stayed there with my people, but then times got so that they were afraid slave traders would grab her up, no matter who she was or who she belonged to…They sent her to Ohio by the Underground Railroad. They had good contacts, being Quakers. My father just told me that she made it safe and sound..."

Alexander L. Haight said that after the Civil War had been over for several years, she sent them this photo, but they never heard from her again.

Cleo
Fenwick Library, George Mason University

Looking at the Slave Schedules laid out above, we can see that in 1850 Jacob Haight owned one black female age 21 and one mulatto female age 4. This may be Cleo and her mother. In the 1860 schedule, Alexander Haight (Phebe's husband) owned only 2 slaves—one black male and one mulatto female age 14. The female probably is Cleo, her mother having already gone to Ohio. This indicates that Cleo would have been born around 1846.

Alexander L. Haight gave several interviews to Fairfax County historians, and some additional details emerged, not always consistent. He said that Cleo was bought by Phebe Haight when Cleo was eight years old near Aldie, Virginia. According to Aldie's website, its glory days were after the Little River Turnpike was completed in the early 1800s, and the town became the 4th largest in Loudoun County, "half of the population" being slaves. An article in the November 2015 Smithsonian Magazine (Retracing Slavery's Trail of Tears: America's Forgotten Migration by Edward Ball) explains its importance as a way station along the slave route south. The author talks of coffle gangs of slaves heading west out of Alexandria. "After 40 miles, the Little River Turnpike met the town of Aldie and became the Aldie and Ashby's Gap Turnpike, a toll road. The turnpike ran farther west…Every few miles, [the] chained-up gang came to a toll station…." (see box below). It was only natural that Aldie became a large slave trading center where Phebe could have bought Cleo.

Slavery's Trail of Tears

The Smithsonian Magazine's article by Edward Ball cited in the text tells of the journey of a million African-Americans from the tobacco South to the cotton South by coffle gangs (chain gangs). He talks of them heading west out of Alexandria, moving along at three miles an hour: "People sang. Sometimes they were forced to. Slave traders brought a banjo or two and demanded music. A clergyman who saw a march toward Shenandoah remembered that the gang members, 'having left their wives, children, or other near connections and never likely to meet them again in this world, sang to drown the suffering of mind they were brought into.' "

In interviews, Alexander Haight also said that Phebe gave Cleo her freedom after the Second Battle of Manassas (1862) and sent her to Ohio where her mother, a runaway slave, was living. This fact begs a number of questions. How did the Haights know where Cleo's mother lived and how did they make contacts with groups who could assist Cleo's journey to safety? The fact that they were Quakers, who were fervent abolitionists, probably aided this effort, as confirmed by Alexander L. Haight's interviews. Although there were Underground Railroad networks throughout the country, even in the South, Ohio had the most active network of any other state with around 3,000 miles of escape routes. An online article called "Touring Ohio" gives two reasons why: Ohio was bordered by two slave states, Virginia and Kentucky, and Ohio was closest to Canada. Ohio also had a large Quaker population that was directly involved in moving escaping slaves north, in particular those coming from Virginia.

Many organizations exist to aid people in their search for ancestors who escaped via the Underground Railroad. One is the Ohio Historical Society that operates the National Afro-American Museum and Cultural Center on the campus of Wilberforce College. Wilberforce, although a small community, had seven stations along the Underground Railroad. I contacted the Museum and Cultural Center and sent them the photo of Cleo, but no information has been found there yet. A search for Cleo/Clio in the Federal Census records with a birth date around 1846 yields very few matches, none of which seems plausible.

Epilogue

This is the end of the list of Sully's enslaved that we have been able to document—most of them not all the way to current descendants but far enough to know that they survived and probably had descendants even though undiscovered in our research. This booklet is, therefore, unfinished. The author requests that anyone with knowledge about the subsequent lives of these enslaved contact her at mesansbury@yahoo.com.

www.ingramcontent.com/pod-product-compliance
Lightning Source LLC
Chambersburg PA
CBHW081635250726
48657CB00009B/2897